Praise for James Tolan's RED WALLS...

In RED WALLS, James Tolan brings us a stunning collection that combines compassion, an abiding, underlying sense of loss, and glimpses of a father and a family deeply flawed and deeply human. In these rites of passage (leading off with the unforgettable poem "Chicago 1942," set in that city's stockyards), Tolan takes us with unflinching imagery to our own hungry, angry, conflicted places of the soul—delivering us, finally, "back to family and air."
– Jo McDougall

In these hard-hitting, compassionate poems James Tolan plumbs the emotional depths of male relationships, laying bare the difficult truths. His work will leave you stunned and wanting more.
– Sheryl St. Germain

Jim Tolan's poems in RED WALLS are vessels Mnemosyne would have recognized as just the kinds of work memory poems should be. These are poems taken with an unflinching heart and shaped by a wise and steady hand. In addition, this carefully contained work shows Tolan's gift for line and sentence and trope and music in the crafting of poems. Here is a work you will not tire of reading over and over again.
– Darrell Bourque

To grasp the viscera and wit of James Tolan's collection, RED WALLS, notice that it begins and ends with hogs, "each in a pig-packed car," moving through boys, booze, bricks, and blood: the blood of the body, the blood of the heart, the spill into the street: "There is never justice/ no way to balance carnage with trial/ There is only the meat and what we do / with it, or without, on the killing floor." James Tolan has brought the flesh back to every word.
– Estha Weiner

RED WALLS

Poems by
James Tolan

2011
Dos Madres Press

DOS MADRES PRESS INC.
P.O.Box 294, Loveland, Ohio 45140
www.dosmadres.com   editor@dosmadres.com

Dos Madres is dedicated to the belief that the small press is essential to the vitality of contemporary literature as a carrier of the new voice, as well as the older, sometimes forgotten voices of the past. And in an ever more virtual world, to the creation of fine books pleasing to the eye and hand.

Dos Madres is named in honor of Vera Murphy and Libbie Hughes, the "Dos Madres" whose contributions have made this press possible.

Dos Madres Press, Inc. is an Ohio Not For Profit Corporation and a 501 (c) (3) qualified public charity. Contributions are tax deductible.

Executive Editor: Robert J. Murphy

Book Design: Elizabeth H. Murphy
www.illusionstudios.net

Typset in Adobe Garamond Pro & Playdough

Library of Congress Control Number:
ISBN 978-1-933675-61-9

First Edition

Acknowledgments

Thanks to the publications in which these poems, often in earlier forms, first appeared:

Bellevue Literary Review: "Cemetery Plums"; *Connecticut Review*: "On the Subject of Hogs" (as "Active Shooter Survival Tips") and "Chicago 1942"; *Indiana Review*: "Blood Sport"; *Linebreak*: "Inheritance"; *Margie: The Journal of American Poetry*: "The Purple Crayon," "Red Walls" and "Whiskey and the Rake of Mourning"; *Paterson Literary Review*: "It was the 70s"; *Quiddity:* "Meat Course." "Blood Sport" and "The Purple Crayon" are included in the *Autumn House Anthology of Contemporary Poetry*. "Downstream" is included in *Two Weeks*, Linebreak Press. "Cemetery Plums" is included in *The Best of the Bellevue Literary Review*. "The Purple Crayon," is included in *Family Matters: Poems of Our Families*, Bottom Dog Press. "Blood Sport" is included in *Coffeehouse Poetry Anthology*, Bottom Dog Press.

I would also like to express my gratitude to Holly Messitt, Lois Griffith, Burt Kimmelman, Jason Primm and Myra Shapiro for helping to make these poems better.

To my son Junuh for helping to make me better.

And to Elizabeth and Robert Murphy, for giving these poems ink and light.

in memoriam
Hal Tolan
(1932-2008)

I want to believe
that if I get the story right

we will rise, newly formed,

that I will stand over him again…
only this time I will know

what to say.

--Nick Flynn

Table of Contents

Chicago 1942

after my father

Every day they pulled the boxcars squealing
up to the stockyard gates. Each pig-packed car
contained its own lead hog onto whose back

they'd drop a boy. *Hold on*, they'd bark,
as they slapped its ass and sent me bolting
toward the gates. A bar just over my head,

grab hold and the nickel was mine, miss
and the rest of the hogs would not.
I always held on. What choice did I have?

Blood Sport

1

When I was a boy, my father would tighten
his stomach and invite me to punch him
as hard as I could. Pounding away,
I'd give him my best shot,
again and again. It was useless.
He was invincible, and I was very small.

2

When I turned six, I asked my father
if I could marry Mom when I was older.
He was never home. Why should he care?
He only cocked an eye and laughed.

3

Still a boy, I raced into the bathroom
while my father was shaving
and belted him right in the gut.
He grunted, doubled over,
and I ran like hell to my mom
only to have her demand that I apologize.

4

Back in the bathroom, I told him
I was sorry. He turned to me,
blood trailing down his throat.
I was a man and would marry as I pleased.

It was the 70s

and the carpets
were wall-to-wall. My mother
had a plastic rake
she used daily to keep the nap
of her green shag piled high.

After raking
the sin was to move around
and mash her plush.
For Christ's sake, Jimmy, can't you
stay put in one place?

I just raked.
It was easier to head outside,
even on a January
afternoon already dark, snow
up to my knees,

and nothing
right or wrong to do. My dad
home early
for once found me lobbing
snowballs up

onto the roof.
Whatcha doin'? Mom just raked
the rug. He nodded,
plucked a lump of snow,
squeezed, and flung

a perfect strike
at the bird feeder planted
twenty paces deep
into the yard. Put a nice crack
in the nearside

plate glass,
then packed another tight one
        that smelled faintly
of Luckies and handed it to me.
Have at it, kid. I'll cover you inside.

Downstream

My uncle, my father's sailor brother Tommy,
used to drink a lot, and I loved him for it.
He'd bring me gifts I didn't even know
I wanted—*How & Why* books on Indians,
aircraft, and fish, a drafting set, colored
pencils and pastels, *Classic Comics*, a pen pal
sister from Vietnam.

     He'd teach me, but only
when he was drinking, how quickly an earthworm
could reproduce by slicing one in two,
how to sketch the colors of an autumn field
and weed the wild places behind the sunflowers
with a machete bought on shore leave in Hong Kong.

Otherwise, he'd spend hours alone in his room,
lost within the all too sober memories
of a broken marriage and a child long years gone,
sketching quiet drawings of half-built houseboats,
women in pedal pushers walking along the shore,
children on swings, forever waiting to be pushed.

Fifteen years since his liver finally called it quits,
I look at a photo the size of a business card.
Silly felt hat drooping over his eyes,
he rows downstream, bare-chested and smiling,
toward no place in particular. I sit across
from him now, in no particular hurry to arrive.

Baptism

At the Grayslake Bocce Ball and Gun Club
lakeside seemed the only almost sanctuary
from the intermittent cock and fire,
from the graveled pitch and clink of old men
at their sport.

          A boy too short to shoot
and wary of the water, all that was left
for me was to watch the flutter kick
and loose-armed skull of my father slipping
methodically into the distance,

when someone taught me how to sink, snuck up
behind and chucked me yelping into air.
My legs reeling, arms flapping, astounded
by trajectory and its descent, I dropped
into the drink.

          Like a dancer flung free
of the stage by a wayward god, I waved
goodbye with both arms to the sky and watched
the unmade promise of a life to come
tumble and lurch to pratfall and plop.

Icarus by another's insistence, I sank
without fight to my uncontested death
until my father swooped in and saved me,
plucked me up and plunked me back onto the dock.
I should have been thankful,

            but the way down—
life quieted, every thing became
its own vast moment—the heft of water
wafting me down, my lank and webless feet,
the bubbles born and rising overhead.

It wasn't the dying I wanted so much
as to live like that slow sinking. Yahweh
could have his heavens and Lucifer his flames.
The meek, awaiting their inheritance,
would find no quarrel with me.

            Delivered
back to family and air, I stood,
stunned and dripping before my grandfather,
red handkerchief tied atop his antic brow.
A matador feigning surrender, he dangled

his smart, white towel my way. I dropped my head
and charged him who had dared me not to drown
and now was snickering, *Toro! Toro!*
as he capered cocksure along the dock.

Whiskey and the Rake of Mourning

When my father's father died,
   my daddy didn't cry a bit,
just grabbed a fifth of whiskey and
   a rake all bent to shit

then dragged himself out the back door
   to do what he did best,
work and drink till the drink was done
   and the work was put to rest.

And when he was through what he had done
   was sheer instead of rake.
The lawn, like a black sheep greened,
   was gone for a dead man's sake,

and the earthen wounds left behind
   gathered a still life of waste,
broken rake and broken man,
   blue-nosed and red-faced.

I hauled his hump into the house
   and poured him to the floor.
The dogs licked vomit from his jowls
   then brayed at the backdoor.

If God is love and father too
   then love is a bare bone.
I left the dogs out in the yard
   and him to rouse his hide alone.

Instead he snored and pissed himself
   upon the kitchen vinyl,
slack-jawed his partial from his gums
   and bloomed a toothless smile.

The Purple Crayon

I find a jumbo Crayola in the new used couch—purple
like in *Harold and the Purple Crayon*, the children's book
I once believed was named after my dad,

                      and I'm sixteen
again, driving him home one more last time from the bar
at Ted's Log Cabin, where he's been since lunch, closing in
again on the indoor martini record, double digits no big thing,

when, stopped at the corner of Lewis and Grand, he flings
open his door and lets loose all over the road. No usual
drunken puking, this one's laced with lots of bloody
coagulum, olives, bifocals, and false teeth.

                    I throw
the two-tone Dodge into park, fish his specs and teeth
out of the mess and drive him to St. Therese and two weeks
in detox before the next new lifetime of *Hi, I'm Hal T and I'm. . .*

My dad's story and a crayon, a lie I've been telling for almost
twenty years. My mother was driving. It was one of the few times
she wouldn't go get him by herself.

                      She is the one who dipped
into what his body emptied to rescue the only help he had ever
admitted to needing, she who drove him to the hospital,
who stayed with him despite all those drunken years,
who loved him more than I have ever known how to love.

I'm thirty-two and still want to be the hero, want to be the one
reaching into the retch, the one making the necessary gesture,
not the pimpled boy in the back seat, his mouth hung wide,
unable or unprepared to act, Hamlet still considering the ghost.

I loved my father and did nothing, sat there, hating myself
for loving this chance to see what he'd been hiding and holding
inside all those years, what he'd been watering and drowning in turn.

Red Walls

Where I come from
we take bricks
one by one.

We take them red
and muddied
from the earth.

Where I come from
we take bricks
from the earth.

We take them
one by one.
Where I come from

masons worked.
Ground grew up.
Ate what

they left behind.
Where I come from
bricks got swallowed.

And it's our job
to loose them
from the soil.

Where I come from
each takes his bricks
and builds a wall

to protect what
we've been given,
to make special

those we invite in.
Where I come from
the stank of one city

mixes with others
on the wind
that finds its way.

Where I come from
hunches grow
from safe places

in the soil, and a soul
builds walls to protect
what must not die.

Where I come from
walls are a kind of flesh
and it's a blessing

to be invited in.
Where I come from
a wolf blows

hot against
the walls all day
and bricks are how

we build a home.
Where I come from
is red bricks from here.

Inheritance

My Grandpa Evo had a special fork
whose tines bent out wide to accommodate
as much scungilli pasta as he could fit
into his wide Italian mouth. I can still
see him shoveling it in, slurping
and licking his lips, slugging Fortissimo
and laughing, smiling at all of us,
his family, before him at tables spread
out across the yard. Sunday dinner,
my mouth open wide in compagnia
di comari, panting with laughter,
I see him in their eyes. Who can be
alone, chi sarebbe solo, among so many?

Filched

Is that vintage? they ask.

It was my dad's, I say, and think of a thirsty man for whom that word meant only a crack about drink, *Gimme a tall one of your finest vintage!*

I found it among tie pins and cufflinks in his top drawer, filched it years before I knew the word,

> when I thought only that I wanted something beautiful and ruined,

> something I could take from him who knew work and the bar better than home.

Crystal scratched, leather dry and stitching frayed, he never noticed it was gone, or else he never said.

From his dresser to the carved wooden box of tattered treasures I buried inside my hand-me-down chest,

> until the no more of him sent me rooting for some relic I could hold.

Glass polished and gears set right, new band strapped to my wrist.

Vintage?

It's beautiful, they say.

It was my dad's, and I let them assume, inheritance or gift,

> that he was a man of taste who shared it with his son.

Let others believe I was offered what I stole.

The Big Sleep

Read it on the Greyhound back before I saw Bogart in Marlowe's clothes,

> before the old man bought the Buick,

> before he changed to dust,

> before my mother scattered him along the highway to Lake Mead beside a scrubby desert tree.

> Before I didn't buy the whiskey,

> before I didn't hoist a glass,

> before I didn't tell the grandson he had never seen,

my father died, not knowing what names went with what faces.

Some hospital joe wheeled him down the long, white hall, while Santa Anas spilled desert across the town.

> While I ducked the rain in Brooklyn, collar against the storm, sodden strangers plunging with me to the train, an ambulance drove him slowly to where the fires blaze, hot enough to roast flesh and bone to scrap and ash.

> While undertakers readied to fit him for the flames, I taught the book that I had plucked from the rack beside his Lazy Boy one Thanksgiving home from school.

He told me to take it if I wanted.

He was done, tired of Chandler anyway.

On a fall day in Vegas, strong winds whipping in,

tourists went on laying down their bets,

showgirls continued powdering their breasts,

and the Lake Mead carp still churned and flopped over
each other, rubbery lips agape, for the popcorn thrown
their way.

Meat Course

The fork rising to my mouth is something more
than etiquette, more than its exquisite balance
and tapered tines.

It is the tool I employ to nourish my fatted flesh,

> the four-pronged stake that carries the
> remains of another whose life becomes
> my own,

> a pitch fork diminished in the service
> of we who cull sacrifice from a menu
> of palatable tropes,

> the minor edifice of civility we impose
> against the plain necessity of death and
> the digestion of its formidable corpse.

A Penniless Piece of Spent Fashion

Who wears my father's face today,
a man miscast before the weather,
rain-splattered, unsure that he is loved?

Who huddles beneath the cold and gray
as north wind bitter slants sharp rain
against the tattered sway of him?

Who wants dry clothes, stiff drink to warm
and unweary his besotted bones,
an ear to fill with liquored yarn?

Who on grim earth alone would wage
a moment's hope on a needle's-eye
chance of resurrection? The son,

whose father forsaken stands, specter
of a man, begging each mortal hand
for what small mercies fall his way,

whose cup of coins becomes his wine,
his heart as mine, faithless and forlorn,
forgetful of what follows rain,

who shades the sun's return—forgiveness
and the muddy-footed crow sent to claw
some clay of hope from life interred,

who finds land the too-white dove demurred
and knows this rain-cloaked creature, famished
and loosed to squalor, whose bloodshot teeth,

whose tartared gaze, I catch before I crush
a twenty into his hand. Rummy eyes,
the crusted corners of his lucred grin.

Cemetery Plums

One who would offer ripe fruit to the dead
as if knowing their desires, as if believing
desire still lived in them, would know
how tangible remains the memory of its juice

across the mouth and chin and sliding
along the tongue. Do not be misled.
The dead miss life more than we miss them,
their loss more than equal to our forgetting

and our grief. And a bowl of fruit offered
in their name returns to them as the memory
of a mouth rapt in joy around moist and living
flesh. Who among the dead does not long

for the sun-wet meat of a smooth-skinned plum,
the bitter sweetness of its pitted heart?

On the Subject of Hogs

(after D. Gordon Kelly)

When surrounded, their first response
is to group, tails together, facing
the aggressor, fighting as a unit.

When the guns report, they learn
from every fallen comrade.

The first are felled between the eyes,
and the rest no longer will face off
directly but maintain aggression

from a flanking position. The next
are shot behind the ear and the others

face nose away in the farthest corner
from a shooter. There is never justice,
no way to balance carnage with trial.

There is only the meat and what we do
with it, or without, on the killing floor.

About the Author

James Tolan is the author of two previous chapbooks *Whiskey and the Rake of Mourning* (Deadly Chaps 2011) and *Fresh Fruit and Gravity* (Far Gone Books 1997). He is an associate professor of English at the City University of New York and the co-editor, along with Holly Messitt, of the forthcoming *New America* (Autumn House Press) an anthology of contemporary literature.